short

long

hard

How you can help

First steps with ladybird *sorting and opposites* will help young children to describe the world around them. Appealing photographs of children and everyday objects will help your child to talk about similarities and differences.

- Enjoy talking about the photographs together. How many teddies can you see on the page? Are they the same or different?

- Encourage your child to compare the sizes of his* toys. Which is the biggest ball? Which is the smallest brick he can find?

There are lots of other ways you can help your child to learn about sorting and opposites. He could sort buttons or beads by colour, shape or size.

Use nursery rhymes like the *Grand Old Duke of York* or *Jack Sprat* to talk about opposites. It's also fun to compare family members to find out who is the tallest, or who has the smallest feet.

*To avoid the clumsy 'he/she',
the child is referred to throughout as 'he'.

Ladybird would like to thank Priscilla Hannaford, freelance editor on this series.

A catalogue record for this book is available from the British Library

Published by Ladybird Books Ltd
27 Wrights Lane London W8 5TZ
A Penguin Company

2 4 6 8 10 9 7 5 3 1

© LADYBIRD BOOKS LTD MM

LADYBIRD and the device of a Ladybird are trademarks of Ladybird Books Ltd

sorting and
opposites

by Lesley Clark
photography by Garie Hind

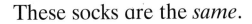

These socks are the *same*.

same

But these socks are *different*.

different

Are these slippers the same?

Are these slippers the same or different?

*Use practical everyday situations, such as tidying up, dressing and playing, to help your child explore things that are the **same** and things that are **different**.*

Teddy bears, teddy bears –
just the same!

same

different

The elephant is *big*, but the mouse is *little*.

big

little

Look at your toys.

Are they all different sizes?

Talk to your child about his own toys. Can he find one that's **big**? *Can he find one that's* **little**?

The bear with the blue and yellow bowl is *large*. The bear with the yellow bowl is *middle-sized*.

large

middle-sized

The bear with the green bowl
is *small*.

small

These things are *cold*…

cold

and these are *hot*.

hot

NEVER touch or go near hot things on your own.

Talking about these pictures of hot things will help your child to understand that they are dangerous and can hurt.

Jenny and her doll have their eyes open. They are *awake*.

awake

Jenny and her doll have their eyes shut. They are *asleep*.

asleep

This glass is *empty*.

empty

Fill it up with juice – now it's *full*!

full

Sally's bucket is *heavy*!

heavy

Now her bucket is *light*!

light

Play water games at bath times, filling and emptying lots of different sized containers.

Look at the children, all in a row –
one, two, three, four.

Who is the *tallest*?

Who is the *shortest*?

shortest

tallest

Children love being measured. Keep a height chart in your child's bedroom as a visual reminder of how much he's grown.

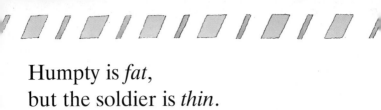

Humpty is *fat*,
but the soldier is *thin*.

thin

fat

The beanbag is *soft* to sit on.

The rock is *hard*.

soft

hard

Where would you rather sit?

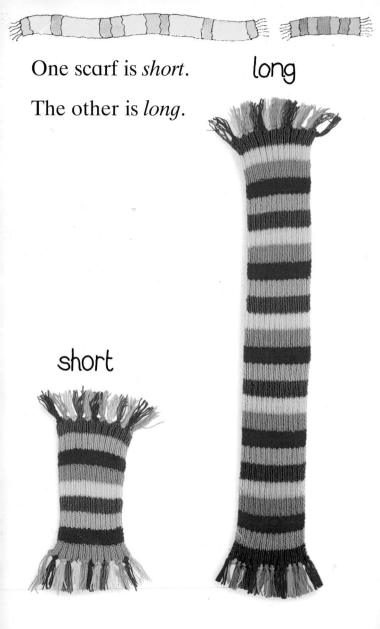

One scarf is *short*.

long

The other is *long*.

short

Emma's hair is short, but Laura's hair is long.

short   long

Is your hair short or long?

*Look for other **long** and **short** things in the photograph. Emma has short sleeves, short socks, etc. Laura has long versions of the same things.*

Climb up to the *top* of the ladder…
one, two, three!

top

up

Whoosh... down to the *bottom*,
quick as can be!

down

bottom

Get *on* the bike...
one, two, three – go!

on

One, two, three – stop!
Now it's time to climb *off*.

off

Open the door and say...

Hello!

open

Close the door, now it's time to go.

Goodbye!

closed

first steps with ladybird

First steps with ladybird is a range of mini readers, activity books and flash cards designed to develop the essential early skills of children aged 2 and upwards.

Mini readers

These durable hardback books use photographs and illustrations to introduce important early learning concepts.